I dedicate this book to my mom, dad, step-dad, brother, sister, and all the teachers that I've had.

Hair Twirlers and Pullers: FOR KIDS (by a kid)

Author: Jack Macallum Malloy

(with a little help from his mom)

It's hard having this habit. I know how you feel.

When I twirl or pull my hair out, I don't always know I am doing it.

Even when I do know I am doing it, I don't always feel like I can control my hands and they pull even when I don't want them to pull.

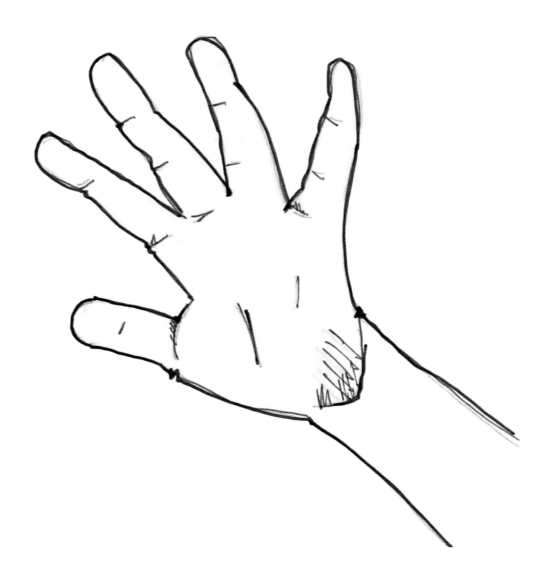

If I know I am going to pull but hesitate to try to stop myself, sometimes my fingers kind of tingle.

That makes it harder to not pull.

Sometimes when I pull my hair out I feel it and it hurts.

Some spots on my head don't hurt and I don't really feel it so I keep pulling it out.

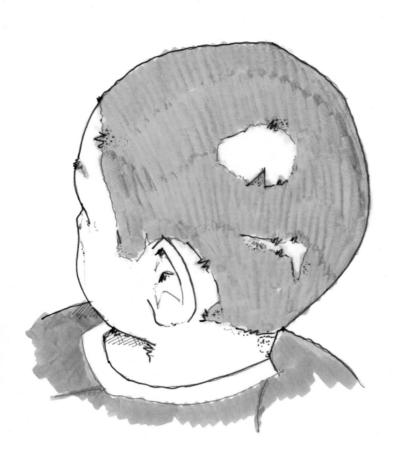

People don't understand why it doesn't hurt and I don't know either, but it doesn't hurt like people think it would hurt.

I know it is not my fault and I cannot control it.

It's not your fault, either.

Don't feel bad about yourself because you are you and everyone has habits. We just have a habit more people can see even when we are not actually doing it.

I don't always know how to stop, but I do know I pull my hair out more when I am tired.

I do it when I am worried or nervous, too.

Twirling and pulling my hair distracts me and takes away some of the worry.

Sometimes I don't know why I do it because I am just reading or playing ball and I feel fine.

It's just my habit and my hands are used to doing it.

Remember that most people have habits.

Some people
bite their nails

Suck their thumb

Crack their
knuckles

Chew on pencils

Tap
their
fingers

Some people just stop their habits and other people need help with their habits to be able to stop.

Most kids can't stop their habits easily and there is no one special thing that helps all kids break their habit.

There are ways to help though, and things you can try.

Some things I do are:

Keep my
hands in
a rhythm
clapping
or moving

or

play with squeeze balls.

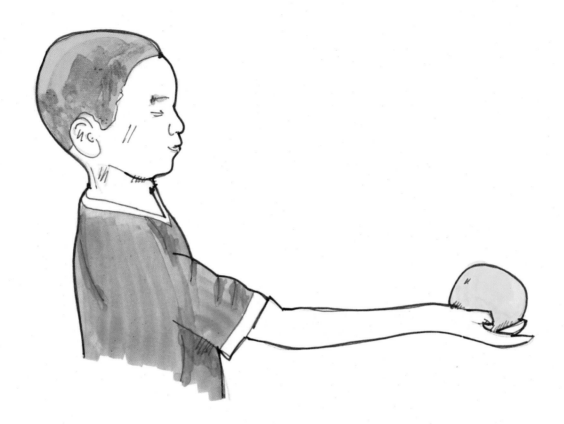

Play catch with a soft ball. This works really well if I start to pull and my mom plays, "Think fast" with me. I have to catch the ball so my hands cannot reach my hair!

Wear a hat--- even my teacher lets me wear one in class at school!

Bounce a small bouncy ball.

Play with string.

Wear a special bracelet for my fingers to play with.

I also have a secret password and "sound" reminder that my mom and friends can say to let me know I am pulling when I don't know I am doing it so I can try to stop.

Sometimes I get an interesting hairdo, like a Mohawk, that I don't want to pull because I want to keep it that way.

Other times I get a really short one that is hard to pull so my fingers don't like it as much and find other things to do.

I know you think you are alone if you have this habit but there are a lot of kids like me that have this habit, too.

We just don't live by each other
to be able to see each other and
know that we aren't alone.

It's not fair and it can make you feel sad sometimes, especially when you don't know why you do it and cannot stop.

Just try to remember that there isn't a good way to help kids stop right now, so just keep trying the best you can.

Everyone likes you and loves you just the same.

Even though it's hard having this habit, remember it's not your fault and you aren't "bad", you are just you and that is actually good!

Jack wrote this book when he was 9 years old. He was born in Kodiak, Alaska and lives in Salem, Oregon most of the year and Kodiak, Alaska, in the summer. He has one older brother, Sean, and one younger sister, Anny. He is a star football player, exceptional reader, and a math whiz. Jack started twirling his mom's hair when he was just 18 months old and that was the beginning of Jack's hair twirling and pulling. As Jack got older, his mom read every book she could find about hair pulling but almost all were for adults with just a chapter or two about how to help kids. Doctors said he would likely grow out of the habit and treatment options were very limited for kids his age. One day, Jack asked, "Mom, are there any kids like me? Did someone make a book about it?" Jack's mom said there were likely millions of kids like him but she had not been able to find a book just for kids. "If there is no book, then who will make one for kids like me?" Jack asked. "You can write one, Jack. You know just what to say to kids like you," his mom replied. Jack smiled and said, "There wasn't one for me but I can write one for the other kids so they know they are not alone." Jack is a boy of his word and this is his book for all the other kids like him.

Made in United States
Orlando, FL
31 March 2022

16343073R00027